Going Shopping With God

"Bringing God Into Everyday Life Situations"

Sylvia Bryden-Stock

Author's Tranquility Press
ATLANTA, GEORGIA

Copyright © 2023 by Sylvia Bryden-Stock

All rights reserved. No part of this publication may be reproduced, distributed, or transmitted in any form or by any means, including photocopying, recording, or other electronic or mechanical methods, without the prior written permission of the publisher, except in the case of brief quotations embodied in critical reviews and certain other noncommercial uses permitted by copyright law. For permission requests, write to the publisher, addressed "Attention: Permissions Coordinator," at the address below.

Sylvia Bryden-Stock/Author's Tranquility Press
3800 Camp Creek Pkwy SW Bldg. 1400-116 #1255
Atlanta, GA 30331, USA
www.authorstranquilitypress.com

Ordering Information:
Quantity sales. Special discounts are available on quantity purchases by corporations, associations, and others. For details, contact the "Special Sales Department" at the address above.

Going Shopping with God Bringing God Into Everyday Life Situations / Sylvia Bryden-Stock
Paperback: 978-1-962492-16-4
eBook: 978-1-962492-17-1

DEDICATION

I am dedicating this book to my Heavenly Father, his son Jesus and the Holy Spirit who are my strength and guides throughout each day and have taught me how to listen to the "inner" voice of God to direct my step.

Table of Contents

INTRODUCTION i
1-*"BUMBLING ALONG"* IN LIFE 1
2-A NEW APPROACH 3
3-SHOPPING WITH GOD 7
4-HOW TO FOLLOW THE HOLY SPIRIT'S NUDGES 12
5-MAKING DECISIONS WITH GOD 15
6-MAKE IT DAILY LIFE PRACTICE 20
7-GOD WANTS TO SHARE EVERY EXPERIENCE 24
8-WALK IN THE POWER OF GOD.. 28

INTRODUCTION

A scripture comes to mind in the New Testament in the book of Philippians. In verse 19 we read *"But my God shall supply all your need according to His riches in glory by Christ Jesus."*

It brought to mind the famous evangelist George Muller who was an evangelist in Bristol in the UK in the early 1800's. He is known for founding many orphanages and schools. He humbly testified to God's miraculous provision for thousands of children and his story can inspire our faith in God today.

Here is snippet from his story—

Night was falling over the harbour of Bristol, England, and in the orphanage founded by George Müller and his wife, the children were getting ready for bed. George was working in his study when his wife arrived with alarming news. "We're out of milk," she said. "There isn't enough for the morning oatmeal."

George laid aside his pen. This wasn't the first time that money needed to buy food and other supplies was tight. The Müllers took in their first group of thirty girls in 1836, and their orphanage now housed over a hundred. From the first George remained resolved never to ask for funds from people or to borrow money. He went to God alone for every need, trusting wholly in the Lord's faithfulness and provision.

The pastor rose from his desk and reached for his wife's hand. "Mary," he said, "let us pray." Two orphanage employees joined them, and together they made their humble yet necessary request to God. Tiny, helpless mouths were depending on them for sustenance. "Be assured, if you walk with Him and look to Him and expect help from Him," George reminded them afterwards, "He will never fail you."

Someone knocked on the door. Mary hurried to answer, returning to the study a moment later. She handed her husband an envelope. "It's a letter, George. Hurry up and open it."

Enclosed was a sum of money, more than enough for the milk. Within minutes, two more letters arrived with money and pledges of support.

This immediate and abundant response to prayer had become a typical experience for Müller. After he came to faith and started meditating seriously on the Bible, he determined to simply trust God at His Word. As a pastor, he decided to live without a salary, relying only on money given to him. George learned to pray faithfully from his heart, asking His Father to move the hearts of men so that they would supply him and his family with what they needed to survive.

Taken from Inspiring Stories by Guideposts.org

My! Such absolute trust in God for his daily supply. I have read his story and been both humbled and inspired. Notice that he would always go to God when there was an urgent need, asking God to "move the hearts of men" to supply. Also, he was seeking God's help with *needs* and not *wants*.

In the scripture above it tells us that God will supply All our Needs. However, I do not believe that our God is like a vending machine.

Tell God what you want and then He will immediately drop your request into your lap!

It takes courage to walk like George Muller, but I do hope this book will help you trust God more – know that He will never let you down.

CHAPTER 1
"BUMBLING ALONG" IN LIFE

How often do you muddle through life and struggle finding that each day seems to be a series of disasters?

How often you wish you had done things differently? Hindsight, it is said, is a great gift!

I lived many years of my life wishing that I had made better decisions or stopped and thought a bit before jumping into something.

It can be so easy to wake up each day and grab a coffee, rush into the day from a place of stress and worry about how you will get through the day. Especially if you have kids to get to school and then you are off to the challenges of the "daily grind".

When I was in nursing training, we had to be on duty by 7:30 a.m. for a morning shift and I could get up, get dressed, go to the canteen, and eat a cooked breakfast and make it to the ward to commence a very busy shift in a maximum of 35 minutes! I have often wondered how I managed it! Most of all—where was God at the beginning of my day, even for a few minutes?

What is interesting is that my upbringing in the charismatic faith had taught me about the importance of having time with God before starting the day and making him first place so that we can be guided safely through stressful times. It says in Proverbs chapter 3 verses 1 and 2 (NIV)—

My Son do not forget my teaching but keep my commands in your heart. For they will prolong your life many years and bring you peace and prosperity.

Then in verses 5 and 6 we read—

Trust in the Lord with all thine heart and lean not on your own understanding. In all your ways submit to him and he will make your paths straight.

Do you have moments where the Holy Spirit is giving you a nudge about something, and you ignore it. It could be a protective warning or a challenge to take a step of faith and be guided to a positive outcome.

Over the next few chapters I am going to share the power of listening to the inner voice of God, those Holy Spirit nudges and the benefit of daily walking in this way.

It took me many years of learning the hard way and making mistakes to realise that the day is best started and walked through with God to help with challenges.

Jesus said in Matthew chapter six some powerful things about not worrying about day-to-day things but to seek God first and everything will follow!

Matthew chapter 6 verse 33 (NIV)—

"But seek first his kingdom and his righteousness, and all these things shall be added unto you."

CHAPTER 2
A NEW APPROACH

It is very interesting how Science and the Bible are so connected through neurological study of the power of the mind to influence Brain tissue and neuropathways.

Recently I came across a Dr Caroline Leaf, a Christian, who has now had 20-30 years of research approved that show how thoughts and the mind influence brain circuits and our overall health. In her book titled "Switch on Your Brain she states—

Science concept – Through our thoughts we can be our own micro surgeons as we make choices that change the circuits in our brains. We are designed to do our own brain surgery and rewire our brains by thinking and by choosing to renew our minds.

For many years there have been books and courses on "the power of positive thinking" and other mind enhancing materials to assist with creating a more joyful and enhanced life. It has been shown that by regular repetition of phrases and bringing in new habits, change can take place with re-wiring the brain neuron circuit for success.

More from DR Caroline Leaf for you—

Our choices – the natural consequences of our thoughts and imagination – get "under the skins" of our DNA and turn certain genes on and off, changing the structure of the neurons of the brain. So, our thoughts, imagination, and choices can change the structure and function of our brains on every level: genetic, epigenetic, cellular, structural, neurochemical, electromagnetic, and even subatomic. Through our thoughts, we can be our own brain surgeons as we make choices that change the circuits in our brains.

I spent many years learning the "holistic" mind changing principals and enjoyed improvement in how I saw life and becoming much less of a victim, along with claiming my own personal power.

However, there was a missing link. Brought up in the Pentecostal faith arena, I gave my life to Jesus at a Billy Graham meeting in London at aged 10 years and valued my spiritual new birth into God's family as well as then receiving the baptism of the Holy Spirit.

I carried that power with me over the years but had a time where the enemy lured me to the holistic arena. I never lost sight of Jesus but was in a compromising walk for a number of years.

Until a light dawned, God called me 100% back to him and then began to show me what true "renewing of the mind" was and how walking with him would truly guide my life according to his plan and purpose for me.

It says in Proverbs chapter 23 verse 7—

For as a man thinketh in his heart so is he

Isn't it wonderful how science is realizing what was written in the Word of God thousands of years ago?

In the beginning God carefully spoke into being the world and then created mankind with a thinking brain.

If we are made in the image of God, then we would have originally been created to have the thinking power of God.

It is through the curse that wrong thinking developed and therefore negative results in life have developed over time.

When Jesus came down as a man and sacrificed His life for us, He destroyed the power of the curse in our lives. Once we become a re-aligned member of God's family through Jesus' death and resurrection inviting him to be Lord of our life, we can access all the benefits that God offers as we renew our thinking in line with God's thoughts.

Paul writes to the Roman church about the key to an empowered life as Christians in *Romans chapter 12 verse 2* when he says—

And be not conformed to this world: but be transformed by the renewing of your mind, that ye may prove what is that good and acceptable, and perfect, will of God.

As our minds are renewed on a day-to-day basis, we will begin to hear God speaking to us through the Holy Spirits nudges and sometimes even a "thought voice" which will help in every-day situations.

Life will be so much more fun and less stressful when you "walk with God", asking for, and working on the renewing of the mind.

Are you thinking God empowered thoughts or Enemy influenced negative and destructive thoughts?

Why not stop right now, where you are and tell God that with the power of the Holy Spirit and the Name of Jesus you wish to begin "renewing your mind" and living in the overcoming power he offers you!

> *Finally, brothers, whatever is true, whatever is honourable, whatever is just, whatever is pure, whatever is lovely, whatever is commendable, if there is any excellence, if there is anything worthy of praise, think about these things. What you have learned and received and heard and seen in me—practice these things, and the God of peace will be with you.*
>
> ***-Philippians 4:8-9***

CHAPTER 3
SHOPPING WITH GOD

When we are living totally from the influence of our earthly carnal mind, it is amazing how many times we can fall into the enemy's trap!

When I had a time of not even thinking about being led by the Holy Spirit, was when I made some really dumb decisions, especially during challenging times.

How many women can relate to "retail therapy" for example?

Maybe some of you guys may be guilty as well! Not necessarily the same as us girls who can get a real buzz out of a new garment for the wardrobe, that when you pull it out to wear, realise that it was a total waste of money – even though it was in the sales – and you couldn't possibly wear it! I do hope it at least went to a charity clothing donation!

I recall a wardrobe clear out of someone's clothes who had passed away. There was a whole wardrobe full of clothes that still had the sales label on and just gathered dust!

Imagine going shopping under the guidance of the Holy Spirit?

Imagine just trusting God for even day-to-day items that will satisfy and bring joy as well as meet ones need?

After all the Apostle Paul writes in *Philippians 4 v 19*—

But my God shall supply all your need, according to His riches in glory by Christ Jesus.

Notice he says ALL our needs, not just some of our needs!

What! I hear you thinking. Is God really interested in our day-to-day budgeting for things like food and clothing?

I am going to share a few personal stories from my own life journey as I began and continue to walk with God on a daily basis. How I began to "shop with God".

In the gospel of Luke chapter 11 Jesus reminds us to trust God for daily provisions. When we walk with God as first place, our provision will be given us. In verse 31 he says—

But rather seek ye first the Kingdom of God and all these things shall be added unto you.

Matthew Ch.6 v 32-34 clearly states—

[32] For the pagans run after all these things, and your heavenly Father knows that you need them. [33] But seek first his kingdom and his righteousness, and all these things will be given to you as well. [34] Therefore do not worry about tomorrow, for

tomorrow will worry about itself. Each day has enough trouble of its own.

SO – here we go—

It was a typical evening at home in my flat and I was having challenging times financially. There was food in the refrigerator but not a lot of good protein foods in there, or the freezer. As I peered in them both wondering what to create for supper, it was like an inner voice spoke and said, "Go to the village supermarket!" "What!" my thoughts responded. "That is SO expensive. Why would I want to go there?". Once again, this thought voice spoke and I ignored, but, after a third time I decided to listen and take notice.

My earthly mind doubted very much that I would be purchasing anything, but three times being told made me sit up and take notice.

As I entered the store, there stood the bargain shopping trolley, So I decided to check it out. My oh My! Reduced way down to UK fifty pence were three large packs of Cod Fillet that could be frozen plus at least three packs of cherry tomatoes at the same price! Nobody else was interested so I grabbed my amazing bargain which cost me a total of UK £3.00 against a normal total of around £20.00! The cod fillets were large enough to make two meals each, six meals in all, and the tomatoes fed me for a week. Isn't God Great!

Then there is another wonderful outcome as a result of listening to the Holy Spirits nudge.

My husband was in care at this time and, being a snappy dresser, loved to wear coordinated colours. One of his favourite jumpers was a rich red cable knit jumper which looked really great on him.

Now, just to illustrate also how God listens to us when we are walking with him daily, here is what happened next. I said to him

"You would look lovely wearing a sky-blue cable knit jumper, just like the red one." Not a popular item at the time.

Thinking no more of it and not chasing around searching for one, life continued. One day whilst in town I went to the mall basement to have a drink and chill for a little while. Adjacent to the food court was a store that sold designer unwanted clothes for a "reasonable price".

The Holy Spirit gave me a nudge like before "Go into T K Max". Well, I was not up for buying or browsing that particular day but, here we go for the second and third time "Go into T K Max".

Like the previous incident I decided I had best obey and was drawn to the back wall of the men's section where there stood a clothes rack with an assortment of clothing hanging. As I walked over, like being guided there, I could see some jumpers and smack bang in the middle of the rack was—

A SKY-BLUE CABLE KNIT JUMPER, MY HUSBAND'S SIZE AND ONE ONLY!

God had heard what I said to my husband and prepared harvesting angels to be ready and arrange for my being in town on the right day at the right time!

It is all too easy to ignore the nudges of the Holy Spirit to our cost, but when we listen the benefits are wonderful.

Think about Abraham for a moment in the book of Genesis. God promised him that he and Sarah would give birth to a son although they were barren at the time and a good age – around 100 years old and well past conceiving. Worried about it happening Abraham took things into his own hands, on Sarah's advice and slept with the maidservant which produced Ishmael and thus began trouble that the lineage still has today. Gods plan did happen in due course but forcing the issue caused major issues.

See *Genesis Chapters 16, 17 and 21*

Remember when Peter listened and obeyed Jesus' command after toiling all night for fish? He caught such a heavy load that it needed two boats to bring it in.

See *Luke Chapter 5 verses 4 -9.*

It pays to get a close relationship with God and listen to the voice of the Holy Spirit. Life's trials might just be a little more easily surmounted.

Have you ever gone shopping for something, and they are out of stock? "We are expecting a delivery in two weeks' time!" Oh, the frustration. The earthly mind kicks in and like Abraham and Sarah you decide that you can't wait, and waste time rushing here and there to get something better, but deep down you really want the item that needs a little waiting time.

I have done this myself numerous times over the years and only ended up exhausted with frustration at not getting what I want at my time! Also not considering whether God desires I need it!

If we are going to let God into every aspect of our life, then we must trust that his timing is perfect and that maybe we are being taught a lesson in patience.

If we desire to walk with God daily, then we must allow the Holy Spirit to guide us. It might mean we take totally different action to what we had intended, or a meeting that will move our life calling forward has to be re-scheduled. We need to be at peace about these things and fully hold on to the knowledge that as I say -

"Everything IS in Divine Order". And "This or Something Better according to your Divine Plan for me"

CHAPTER 4
HOW TO FOLLOW THE HOLY SPIRIT'S NUDGES

So how do I know I am hearing the Holy Spirit speaking to me?

How can I walk my life in partnership with him all the time?

Jesus promised us the comforter when he had to leave the earth. The gospel of *John chapter 14 verses 16 / 17* is where he talks about the Holy Spirit—

And I will pray the Father and he shall give you another Comforter, that he may abide with you forever; Even the Spirit of truth; whom the world cannot receive, because it seeth him not, neither knoweth him not: but ye know him; for he dwelleth with you and shall be in you.

In verse 26 he says—

But the Comforter, which is the Holy Ghost, whom the Father will send in my name, he shall teach you all things, and bring all things to your remembrance, whatsoever I have said unto you.

When we become born again the Holy Spirit lives within our spirit. The closer we get to God through our relationship with Jesus, he will increase the Holy Spirit manifestation in our life. I heard a minister speaking about being guided by the Holy Spirit and assured that the more we are familiar with God's word, the more we will recognise what is the nudge of the Holy Spirit.

It can take time to become one with the Holy Spirit and fully know what genuine nudges from the Holy Spirit are.

For me it was a journey of recognising the "gut reaction" that felt right about something, opposed to the opposite.

I recall going to look at a certain make of car: as I sat in the driver's seat something "went off in my Gut" and the initial reaction was to put that car on my wish list. As I considered the inner nudge after some time had passed, I realised that it was not the car for me and never did invest in that particular make and model. I had received a nudge that actually meant that make, and model car was not intended for me. Over the years I have come to be blessed with what I call the voice of God as well as intuitive sensing of the voice of the Holy Spirit.

You can always ask God or Jesus for confirmation that it is them and if you are protected daily with the blood of Jesus and working on having the mind of Christ you will know his voice and be blessed as you follow his calling to do certain things – even day-to-day tasks. In the gospel of *John chapter 10 verse 27* Jesus says—

My sheep hear my voice, and I know them, and they follow me.

He is the shepherd talking about his flock. As those born again with a personal relationship with him, we are his flock and should want to follow his guidance. He used that illustration as many were employed as shepherds in his day.

So I encourage you to work at daily walking close with Jesus through prayer and study of God's Word (the Bible). Make it a daily habit to start the day right and you will grow into knowing the Holy Spirit nudges and have an exciting life, where your needs are met in unusual ways.

See Philippians chapter 4 verse 19—

But my God shall supply all your need according to his riches in glory in Christ Jesus.

Be prepared to be nudged to do what seem bizarre things but follow through and the results will be amazing for you!

I love living my life by following the voice of Jesus and Holy Spirit Guidance. Plus knowing that if circumstances take a different route than Your Mind had thought out, it is for a purpose. I have missed being involved in many a motorway accident through what seemed delay tactics with my getting organised to leave, only to find out that the twenty-minute delay on leaving was the Holy Spirit protecting me from being involved in a major car accident!

Let renewal of your mind to the Mind of Christ be your goal – Romans chapter 12 verse 2

And be not conformed to this world but be ye transformed by the renewing of your mind, that ye may prove what is that good, and acceptable, and perfect will of God.

CHAPTER 5
MAKING DECISIONS WITH GOD

Do you like making decisions?

How do you come to decisions in life?

There is a lot of information to be found about decision making from a good old google search!

When you think about it, we have been making decisions since this world began.

Let's go back to the beginning and the very first decision that was made that would influence mankind for time to come. I am talking about the decision made in the Garden of Eden with Adam and Eve – God had told them that there was one tree that they were not to partake of but that all the rest were there's to enjoy. Then the decision came when the serpent(Lucifer) tempted Eve.

Genesis 3:1-6 King James Version (KJV)

3 Now the serpent was more subtil than any beast of the field which the Lord God had made. And he said unto the woman, Yea, hath God said, Ye shall not eat of every tree of the garden?

2 And the woman said unto the serpent, We may eat of the fruit of the trees of the garden:

3 But of the fruit of the tree, which is in the midst of the garden, God hath said, Ye shall not eat of it, neither shall ye touch it, lest ye die.

4 And the serpent said unto the woman, Ye shall not surely die:

5 For God doth know that in the day ye eat thereof, then your eyes shall be opened, and ye shall be as gods, knowing good and evil.

6 And when the woman saw that the tree was good for food, and that it was pleasant to the eyes, and a tree to be desired to make one wise, she took of the fruit thereof, and did eat, and gave also unto her husband with her; and he did eat.

Here Eve was in a position of making a decision. She already knew what God had told them about the trees. Instead of staying with what was God's best advice, she listened to the serpent and made a decision from the perspective he put to her. Then she convinced Adam and "the rest is history" as they say!

They knew they had made a wrong decision, but it was too late to change it. It introduced fear and the downfall of humanity.

Do you make decisions that you regret afterwards?

I have made some really dumb, major decisions in my life. One was getting into a relationship that, although I seemed happy, from soon after the beginning the Holy Spirit was giving me "gut instinct" nudges that I ignored because at that time I, like Eve, was vulnerable to the influence of others. It took a lot of inner work on myself and eventually listening to and following God's way that got me back on track to walking daily with him.

Indecisiveness often links to fear of change, even if you know that you should really seek change. The human thinking mind is either your worst enemy or best friend if it is working with your spirit self.

As Christians we strive to walk 100% with "the mind of Christ" which is given us when we are born again—

...but we have the mind of Christ.

1 Corinthians 2 verse 16

Let this be in you also which was in Christ Jesus

Philippians 2 verse 5

The more we focus on living from "the mind of Christ", the more we will bring God into our decision making.

It makes sense to bring God into every decision we make because he sees all and can help us make the best decisions in life.

It is said, from researching, that there are seven steps to making a decision—

Step 1: Identify the decision. You realize that you need to make a decision...

Step 2: Gather relevant information...

Step 3: Identify the alternatives...

Step 4: Weigh the evidence...

Step 5: Choose among alternatives...

Step 6: Take action…

Step7: Review your decision & its consequences.

This is great advice and will work well in business for example. However, I read a book about intuitive marketing which was following positive gut instinct that may seem crazy but worked.

Suppose we started each day and then throughout the day we took situations to God and asked for his help with getting the right answer for making a decision?

In the book of Proverbs there is a great piece of wisdom —

Proverbs 3:5-6 King James Version (KJV)

5 Trust in the Lord with all thine heart; and lean not unto thine own understanding.

6 In all thy ways acknowledge him, and he shall direct thy paths.

Matthew 6:33 King James Version (KJV)

33 But seek ye first the kingdom of God, and his righteousness; and all these things shall be added unto you.

What great advice for us Christians.

Imagine how different each day would be in life if God was brought into decision making. What does it say in Proverbs? — when you acknowledge God and get out of the programmed earthly mind, he WILL DIRECT YOUR PATHS!!

Believe me I have learned to let God into my decisions and listen to the Holy Spirit guidance but have not fully perfected it yet!

Spending time with God each day will bring you into alignment with his voice and the Holy Spirit nudges and answers you are seeking will manifest for you according to what God considers is the best answer for you. Just trust and believe those Holy Spirit nudges.

Learn to get the earthly thinking aligned to God's thinking. Read your Bible and you will see that he had a big part to play in the decisions the Israelites made. When they listened, all went well. When they ignored God's help things went "pear shaped"!

Jesus relied on God. —

John 14:10 Believest thou not that I am in the Father, and the Father in me? the words that I speak unto you I speak not of myself: but the Father that dwelleth in me, he doeth the works.

In an article I read about decision making for Christians, the very first of seven steps in decision making was – **Direction From God**

So, are you ready to bring God into your decision-making process?

CHAPTER 6
MAKE IT DAILY LIFE PRACTICE

I recall the story of Joshua in the Old Testament who was to lead the people of Israel into the promised land. In Joshua chapter one we read —

8 This book of the law shall not depart out of thy mouth; but thou shalt meditate therein day and night, that thou mayest observe to do according to all that is written therein: for then thou shalt make thy way prosperous, and then thou shalt have good success. 9 Have not I commanded thee? Be strong and of a good courage; be not afraid, neither be thou dismayed: for the LORD thy God is with thee whithersoever thou goest.

Here we see that God told Joshua that he was to meditate on the book of the Law day and night and follow what was written therein to be successful and prosperous. That coupled with courage would eliminate fear, for God was always with him.

Wow! What a promise! Often when I am reading scriptures in the morning one will jump out at me and inspire and direct how I should be living as a follower of Jesus. The more we dig into the messages throughout the Bible, the more we will be able to trust God in daily life situations.

Reading a chapter of the books of Psalms and Proverbs every day is uplifting, as well as giving wisdom on how to live a great life. You will see how King David took all his problems to God and also thanked and praised God for his protection and deliverance.

In the book of James in the New Testament it says —

If any of you lack wisdom, let him ask of God, that giveth to all men liberally, and upbraideth not; and it shall be given him.

James 1:5 | KJV

Where do we find an amazing wisdom resource? In God's Word and especially the book of Proverbs!

In the New Testament Jesus promised a comforter when he had to leave the earth and return to his father in heaven in the form of the Holy Spirit. He said these words to his disciples in John chapter 14 v. 16 –

And I will pray the Father, and he shall give you another Comforter, that he may abide with you for ever;

In verse 26 Jesus refers to the role of the Holy Spirit —

26 But the Comforter, which is the Holy Ghost, whom the Father will send in my name, he shall teach you all things, and bring all things to your remembrance, whatsoever I have said unto you.

So, in this verse we are shown how the Holy Spirit is our great teacher and makes us aware of walking as Jesus taught. He will speak to us through those "gut feelings" we talked about earlier.

When we receive Jesus as Lord of our life, the Holy Spirit enters into our spirit and will speak to us daily if we will listen.,

It is through daily communion with God, Jesus, and the Holy Spirit that we can create a much more powerful life. Even when challenges arise, that intimate walk with God will guide us and bring us through.

What is most important is that we follow the Holy Spirits guidance to the letter and trust for an outcome that is the very best for us, even if it seems weird at the time of asking and receiving answers. God wants to answer our prayers and there is no greater scripture than Mark chapter 11 verses 24 & 25 —

24 Therefore I say unto you, What things soever ye desire, when ye pray, believe that ye receive them, and ye shall have them.

25 And when ye stand praying, forgive, if ye have ought against any: that your Father also which is in heaven may forgive you your trespasses.

If we want to hear God every day, he needs to hear from us and wants to hear our requests for help and guidance EVERY day. He is interested in our earthly life and wants it to be lived from the inside out and attract blessings in every aspect of the experiences we have.

Daily time with God – even a few minutes as well as talking with him about Everything – will develop our hearing from God through the Holy Spirit.

In the verses above Jesus talks about "whatsoever". That means Anything! All he requests from us is to make sure when we come to him, we remember to come with an attitude of forgiveness. Forgiving others and ourselves is a major key to an empowered and blessed life as a Christian.

Daily time with God should include "listening" time as well as the asking. He may guide you immediately or the Holy Spirit will nudge you during the day to take a certain action that will bring answers for you.

The closer we walk with God and allow the power of the Holy Spirit to guide us each day, we counteract the power of the enemy to sneak in and use our mind to worry instead of listening and trust.

For me, I talk to God and Jesus as a friend and family member through my salvation and may say things like —

"OK Jesus, what are we doing today?"

"I need an answer Jesus!"

"Jesus, I love you and all that you help me with".

Sometimes I get a vision of what to prepare for a meal or what clothes to wear. No, I am not living as a robot. I did say sometimes! I just love walking every day with Jesus and the power of the Holy Spirit.

I urge you to start daily walking closer to God and see how your life transforms in all ways.

CHAPTER 7
GOD WANTS TO SHARE EVERY EXPERIENCE

Why do we think that God is not interested in our day-to-day life journey?

Why do we think Jesus is not interested in earthly things since he left the earth?

Let's take a look at Genesis for a starter.

After God had created Adam and Eve what is written about God and his creation?

In Genesis chapter 3 we read how after the temptation of Satan and the covering up of their bodies, Adam and Eve hid in the garden of Eden and when God came to commune with them in the cool of the evening he was calling out to Adam and could not find him. This indicates that there was regular communion between God and Adam and Eve. See *Genesis chapter 3 verses 8 to 10.*

Through the sacrifice of Jesus on the cross we have permission as believers to have intimate communion with God, Jesus, and the Holy Spirit.

Did not Jesus say in *Matthew chapter 28 verse 20* when he commanded his disciples to preach the gospel *"... and lo I am with you always, even unto the end of the world."*

If he is with us ALWAYS, then surely that must mean ALWAYS!! Even in day-to-day life experiences.

All through the bible we are encouraged to walk in close communion with God.

How did Joshua succeed?

In Joshua chapter 1 verse 9 it states —

Have not I commanded thee? Be strong and of a good courage; be not afraid, neither be thou dismayed: for the Lord thy God is with thee whithersoever thou goest. KJV

The more closely we walk with God and bring him into each day, amazing things begin to happen —

- You meet people who are needed to be of help with your earthly assignment.
- Ideas are given to you that will solve challenges.
- Your shopping spree will have unexpected bargains lined up for you.
- An email pops into your inbox from someone you need to communicate with

I literally will go shopping with God for groceries and find totally unexpected bargains that are not usually available at that time of day.

Recently I had an inner Holy Spirit nudge to read the meters and when I went into my account to submit them, I saw that I was heavily in CREDIT!!

A refund was agreed by the company PLUS in a few days a further small refund notice dropped into my email inbox!

In the bible it talks of Gods ministering spirits in Hebrews chapter 1 verse 14 —

Are they not all ministering spirits, sent forth to minister for them who shall be heirs of salvation? KJV

I'm sure God has ministering angels waiting to be called on to help us.

Why is it that, as Christians, we can get so caught up in feeling we should "be strong" when God is ready to help. I love the Scripture in Philippians chapter 4 verse 13 where the apostle Paul says —

I can do ALL things through Christ which strengthens me KJV

Most days on rising. I state this scripture out loud.

It certainly helped whilst journeying with my husband diagnosed with Young Onset Alzheimer's Disease! Especially when energy was needed to get through the day after a night of little sleep!

I was bringing God and Jesus into my daily life and learned the power of doing so.

I certainly needed to allow the Holy Spirit to guide me in how I responded to Alzheimer's Brain Neuron activity.

Are you willing to bring God into everything you do?

It doesn't mean you become God's puppet. It does mean that everyday life can become a more joyous experience for you.

Listening to the Holy Spirit's nudges may challenge you to pace yourself more, plus take moments to relax and dwell in the wonderful presence of the ever-loving Father who loves to commune with his children.

We live in such a fast-paced society that it can become easy to create habits where iPhones and iPads distract us.

How can God communicate and the Holy Spirit guide if all day long emails and texts are being checked.

Do you ever turn your mobile phone / iPad off or on to silent mode?

Is there always music playing or is the TV on?

God wants to share those day-to-day moments. It seems that silence is more of a rarity these days. Remember the verse of scripture in *Psalm chapter 46 verse 10* —

Be Still and Know that I am God

It is in moments of quiet that we will feel his presence that inner guidance nudge OR even the voice of God speaking. When we listen to and follow God's guidance life becomes less stressful.

I am still learning – I'm not perfect; but I do make sure I start the day right, that is, time with God inviting him into my day and giving thanks.

I challenge you, from this moment on, to invite God into your everyday life. Let Father, Son and Holy Spirit walk close beside you.

Talk with them as you would a trustworthy friend. Jesus said – *"Lo I am with you Always…"* He wants you to walk with him as his friend.

CHAPTER 8
WALK IN THE POWER OF GOD

Our God is All Powerful and his power is shown throughout scripture from Genesis to Revelation.

Consider for a moment how God, by calling forth, threw together, in perfect balance the universes and galaxies – some which are still being discovered.

Then God empowered Adam to *"...be fruitful and multiply and replenish the earth..."* in *Genesis chapter 1 verse 28*.

Fast forward to Moses who led the Israelites out of Egypt. It was God's power that gave him the courage to face Pharaoh. Here is what he said to God in *Exodus chapter 3 verse 11 - "Who am I that I should go unto Pharaoh, and that I should bring forth the children of Israel out of Egypt?"*

Then in chapter four, with Moses still feeling inadequate, God showed his power to use an everyday item and work his power through it.

Exodus chapter 4 verses 2 – 4, is where God speaks to the unsure Moses - *"2. And the Lord said unto him, what is that in your hand? And he said, A rod. 3. And he said, Cast it on to the ground. And he cast it on to the ground, and it became a serpent; and Moses fled from before it. 4. And the Lord said unto Moses, put forth thine hand, and take it by the tail. And he put forth his hand, and caught it, and it became a rod in his hand;"*

All through the bible we see how God empowered all manner of people. Look at the Psalmist David for example. I love how he overcame the giant Goliath. He was a short ruddy complexion teenage lad who knew the power of God in daily life as he tended his flock of sheep. He killed a bear and a lion with his bare hands and then rose to the challenge of taking on the Philistine Giant Goliath. In the book of *1 Samuel chapter 17 verses 43 and 47* we read what he says to Goliath —

"Then said David to the Philistine. You came to me with a sword, a spear, and a javelin, but I come to you in the name of the Lord of hosts, the God of the ranks of Israel, Whom you have denied...And all this assembly shall know that the Lord saveth not with sword and spear; for the battle is the Lord's, and he will give you into our hands."

No matter what David went through in life he trusted in God's power to protect and overcome.

Then, if we turn to the New Testament, we see how Jesus worked with his father's power to perform his miracles. He stated in *John chapter 5 verses 19, 20* - *"The son can do nothing of himself, but what he seeth the father do: for what things soever he doeth, doeth the son likewise."*

Having come to earth as a human he had to work with God the father's anointing which released power to do the miracles.

What is amazing is what Jesus said to his disciples before his crucifixion regarding what would be available to believers after he went back to sit at the right hand of God. In John chapter 12 verses 12 – 14 he says *"Verily, verily, I say unto you; He that believeth in me, the works that I do shall he do; and greater works than these shall he do because I go uno my father. And whatsoever ye shall ask in my name, that will I do, that the father may be glorified in the son. If ye shall ask anything in my name, I will do it"*.

Wow! What a statement! That means we can tap into God's power through the name of Jesus!

Why are we not tapping into that power more in our daily lives? It is worth reading *Mark chapter 11 verses 22 – 25*. Here Jesus states that with faith as a grain of mustard seeds – and how tiny is That! – we can speak to our "mountains" and tell them to go into the sea. All he requires of us is to *believe* and *expect* it to come to pass along with a powerful key – *forgive* anyone who needs to be forgiven.

I lived many years without knowing fully this truth. When I realized the power that was available to me, I decided to tap into it and walk in it to my very best every single day.

All throughout the bible, way back to Abraham's time, the power of God was evident in people's lives. Ordinary folks like you and me. All that was required was for them to tap into God's power, be obedient to his instructions, *believe,* and see God work supernatural miracles.

This kind of living has to be worked at daily and we have to let go of the earthly mind set perspective and allow the Holy Spirit to guide. Trust the inner nudges that become more and more powerful that we trust and follow for the great results to occur. In the book of *Romans chapter 12 verse 2*, the apostle Paul writes - *"And be not conformed to this world but be ye transformed by the renewing of your mind, that ye may prove what is that good, and acceptable, and perfect, will of God."*

That takes effort and patience but is worth it to walk daily in God's power. How do you achieve that?

- START THE DAY WITH GOD

- START EACH DAY WITH GRATITUDE

- REJOICE IN WHAT YOU HAVE

- ASK, BELIEVING YOU WILL RECEIVE

- FORGIVE OTHERS AND YOURSELF

Why struggle in life when there is a God waiting to guide and help.

We were never promised a life free of trials, but Jesus tells us he has overcome the world (John 16 verse 33) and that with God All things are possible (Matthew 19 verse 26)

When you know that God is interested in everyday life it becomes a powerful daily walk with him. Jesus gave us the authority of his name and we should use it. In the book of John chapter 14 verses 12 -14 Jesus tells his disciples the following —

12 Verily, verily, I say unto you, He that believeth on me, the works that I do shall he do also; and greater works than these shall he do; because I go unto my Father.

13 And whatsoever ye shall ask in my name, that will I do, that the Father may be glorified in the Son.

14 If ye shall ask anything in my name, I will do it.

That is as they say, straight from the horse's mouth!

The sooner mankind acknowledges the message Jesus gave of forgiveness of wrong doings or sin, and a new spiritual life walking in his power, the sooner we will see lives dealing with all circumstances knowing that with the power of his name we can overcome!!

Start today living your life walking and talking with God about everything and watch life change for you.

www.ingramcontent.com/pod-product-compliance
Lightning Source LLC
LaVergne TN
LVHW040203080526
838202LV00042B/3298